the weight of light

the
weight
of light

poems

gary lemons

Red Hen Press | *Pasadena, CA*

Book layout by Cassidy Trier

Library of Congress Cataloging-in-Publication Data
Names: Lemons, Gary, author.
Title: The weight of light / Gary Lemons.
Description: First edition. | Pasadena, CA : Red Hen Press, [2017]
Identifiers: LCCN 2016048426 | ISBN 9781597090476 (pbk. : alk. paper)
Classification: LCC PS3612.E475 A6 2017 | DDC 811/.6—dc23
LC record available at https://lccn.loc.gov/2016048426

The National Endowment for the Arts, the Los Angeles County Arts Commission, the Dwight Stuart Youth Foundation, the Max Factor Family Foundation, the Pasadena Tournament of Roses Foundation, the Pasadena Arts & Culture Commission and the City of Pasadena Cultural Affairs Division, the City of Los Angeles Department of Cultural Affairs, the Audrey & Sydney Irmas Charitable Foundation, Sony Pictures Entertainment, Amazon Literary Partnership, and the Sherwood Foundation partially support Red Hen Press.

First Edition
Published by Red Hen Press
www.redhen.org

Acknowledgments

I am grateful beyond expression to all the people who contributed along the path of this book's arc through time.

Especially Nick Hill for his willingness to examine and comment and ultimately print out endless versions of the manuscript as it evolved and then recycle these pages into note paper.

Gratitude to John Huey—perhaps my oldest living friend—who was critically involved in the final two edit cycles of *The Weight of Light*—without his sage guidance and fine ear the poems would suffer even more from the irascible nature of the author.

To Norman Dubie—my first teacher, admired poet, dearest of men.

To W. H. Auden for his lovely sestina "Paysage Moralisé" and the quote used in "The Birdbath of Saint Francis."

To my friends and family who are one and the same with enduring gratitude to Anne Jablonski, Xulia Duran-Rodriquez, Christa Pierson, Clint Willis, Carie Garett, Dirk Nelson, Hanno Giulini, Jenny Van West and Erich Schiffmann.

And to Kate Gale, Mark Cull, Selena Trager and Alisa Trager—and especially Reba Nutting—whose editorial insights made this a better book—as well as the other wonderful people at Red Hen Press—thank you—for who you are, what you do, and how well you do it.

Thank you Nöle—for the worlds we've made and are making.

for Nöle—
for the worlds we've made
and are making
from a shared forever

Contents

"... there is an enormous amount of invisible light in the universe that is indistinguishable from darkness until it touches something and only then do we see it..."

—Unknown

"... without either dissection into science, or digestion into art, but with the whole of consciousness, seeking to perceive it as it stands; so that the aspect of a street in sunlight can roar in the heart of itself as a symphony, perhaps as no symphony can: and all of consciousness is shifted from the imagined, the revisive, to the effort to perceive simply the cruel radiance of what is."

—*Let Us Now Praise Famous Men*
James Agee & Walker Evans, 1939

Winter Tides

1

The last thing I remember—
Before they placed the ether rag
Over my face in preparation for cutting
Off the leg now iridescent as an oil spill
At sunrise—is the surgeon's yellow teeth
Clenching the stem of a dead cigarette—

I was pulled through the years
Across a pure white snow by my brothers
And sisters between bare hardwood
Trees cut down by partisans
To build an abatis around the last
Outpost of impossible innocence—

In this safe place we agreed—to
Never grow old—protected by gasmasks
From the toxic fumes of legacy dreams—
We stood without weapons like a forest the years
Approach with hatchets and saws to
Turn wilderness into useful things.

We melted the red snow—
Drank the remnant protein in vows pried
From the tongues of our fallen.

The death of the illusion—bah—
What is that to us who never believed
In the ridiculous theatre of clocks.

2

I awaken in the dirt beside
A young woman with no face below
The nose—she has the most
Beautiful green eyes—as if the forest
Grew out of them into me—as

If there was light—and she rising
Up the stem of her spine
From torn earth into the bloom
Coveted by the harvesters.

Outside the bunker a child
Wrestles with a dog for my lost leg—
One—of course—to sup on it—the
Other for the boot and the lace—

This resembles the tomorrow
We thought to prevent—
Littered with blown luggage
And broken vials and wet needles
Of pine fallen on torn flags
In a darkness lit up by fear.

3

A siren with a lute is singing
Across time to all of us—words
She makes up on the spot—her
Unrehearsed lyrics as beautiful
As the light trapped in the folds
Of her tail—like winter inside a
Sun-drenched rose—

She recites the song of icicles
Melting—the sound of bones
Mending—the words we remember
Long after we come down from mountains
To see we are mountains—

The song has many elements—
Mixing restraint and anger into forgiveness—
And leaf mold in ditches—the patrician
Approval of fathers—the historical
Letters signed when love was
As simple as a vineyard by the sea.

4

The train slows for the whistle
Stop known as death—the broken
Petals of wildflowers still blue

In a frozen meadow under snow
Have little to say about the speed
Of light—only the weight of it.

In the gardens of memory a hemophilic
Ghost juggles two-edged swords
Where even the slightest cut causes
Long-forgotten details like sunlight
On a collarbone to bleed out
Into an unexpected fire that vaporizes
The character known as the self—

What's left after the resistance fails?
The cause now altered by the sacrifice
Of those who died for it—and this is all
The fossils of innocence in the heart will reveal—
The shadows that don't fade at night—
Dragging each other toward hidden light
As the sun goes down.

A Wealth of Little

This is cold—a blue tremble—
The blizzard is over but inside
The snow still falls—

Image 1—my people
Coughing kerosene—walls like eyes
Remembering the panic of livestock
Trapped by fox as the protection of the last
Dog drips over a yellow flame—

This is a vestige of joy—the quiet
Power of mountains
In the eyes of a something consumed
By and for its sacrifice—

Image 2—bodies fragrant
As birth rags—mountains so sharp the sky
Spreads a destitute form of worship
Over an unforgiving silence—

We have nothing and are nothing
But even so understand everything—
This urgency to rise in the night—
This old word for falling snow.

Frontier

She looks—at her hands
Bleeding into the wood
Of the singletree plough—

The crazed furrows behind
Her and the skanky mane
Of the gray mule strapped
To the plough like a whip
To its handle—

There is no evidence
That anything in the immediate
Landscape contributes
Its lard to the occasional crust.

She thinks of her family
In the little sod house
On the horizon—sees smoke
Rising in black plumes
Into a sky playing its old blue song—
Then remembers the cooking
Fire made before the sun
Came up was put out to
Conserve fuel—

She hears the faint whooping
Like a single mockingbird
Defending its night soil—

So far away it might be
An audience in a dream applauding
A better dream—with her skirts
Pulled to her knees she
Runs toward the house—the holstered
Pistol flapping on her hip.

The Comanche
Are done burning
Everything of interest and
So move back to the prairie
Like musicians dragging
Their instruments away
From silence.

It's still. The light fails
From yellow to purple to black.
Then it screams—the light—
As it disappears.

Painted Ponies

The desert is prepared
For anything except rain
And the inevitable consequences
Of an extravagant gift—

One old guy claims he drove
Cattle on the Goodnight-Loving
Trail but it turns out he only
Remembers the journey from
The perspective of a cow—

Past lives are a bitch—
And then you live.

Concerto for Horn and Guitar

It was a lovely but insufficient
Commitment to suck the stranger's
Toes in her mouth then wet them with
The gravy of her disregard—

He wanted more—he wanted
To be like cornbread dredged through
Every drop of her—but this is literature
And something must be saved for the last
Page—something that allows room
In the marginal truth for the tra la la la
Coming from the alert and freshly
Watered violets on the sill—

That's when she noticed the hooks
On the ceiling above the bed hung
With tiny throats that all at once
Delivered a sermon on restraint
And what it means to escape higher
Up a tree with bitten feet and
The strength in tired arms.

She's alone now—brushing
Her long hair into a bucket of milk
As hereditary baldness
And change of life collide
With every stroke—once the bucket
Is filled with what falls out

She will offer the contents
To the narrator watching inside
The mirror—watching the physical
Brushing to make sure there's
An authentic commitment to the story
And not the common falsehoods or easy
Images stroked from the pre-ordained.

If anyone reads this please
Don't think there's an ulterior
Reason for speaking of the boudoir
As a place where zookeepers
Might apply for work—be aware—love
Was hurried into extinction by
Those who covet its wrist bones
To decorate the necks of doctors
Debating the perfect mixture of chemicals
To stop the prisoner's heart—

And who isn't a doctor—who isn't
A prisoner—who isn't about to be executed?
Who hasn't once been loved?

Let's be clear—this is winter—
This is the cold sky shouting
Curses down the megaphone of the stem
At the orphans huddled underground—

This is the mistaken familiarity
Of fruit going bad when exposed to light—this
Is the lullaby sung to the creature
With horns in a frozen trough
Where moonlight is insufficient to
Melt the ice that holds it—

This is the autobiography
Of purple martin wings amplified
All evening into an audible
Requiem for the beautiful instruments
Dangling from the gallows of right now.

Unframed

A child in the forest sits
Atop a downed nurse log
For comfort as well as to
Balance the paper upon
Which she paints a sky
Empty of anything but the washed
Blue of her father's eyes
When he drank enough wine
To shout at dinner.

At first the quiet trees
Manage to absorb—like carbon
Dioxide—the toxic residue
Of childhood dreams but after a while she
Paints a big sun in the middle
Of the washed-out blue sky.

Later at home she trembles
In bed afraid that in her painting The sun is going down.

Tenderness

For Nöle

The man who might be me
Re-creates the streets of his youth
With each step across the plowed
Ground of the farm inherited
From parents worn to death
By weather and bad news.

He remembers most of it—the faces
Of strangers in the stream
Of a passing bus—the iodine sky
Saturated with fired guns—the woman
Across the bar glancing away when
He stared too long for courtesy.

There were lessons then—a few learned
Well and most of them not at all—that break
The shovel used to dig them now.

The one I learned best looks across
The table and smiles with both hands
Around mine—draws me across the planted fields—
Closer over coffee songs—whispering—
One kiss can save the world.

Conquistadores

Sitting on his horse overlooking
The siege of New York City
The barbarian commander signals
With tentacles at the catapults
To launch huge boulders
At the institutions of high finance.

The horse is a blue roan
With a black mane and tail
And has carried skeletons
Back and forth between the mother
Ship and the planet and is
Accustomed to the twang of siege
Engines so when it relieves
Itself it's not from fear but—
As a warhorse—to contribute something
To the enemy's confusion.

The bankers watch the stone
In mid-air coming slowly across
The sky like the meteor brontosaurs
Might have registered briefly
Before the Smithsonian opened—

Barbarians have no heart
So for them this is not an emotional
Experience—it's just the end of money—
The end of barter—the end of

Intersections between faith and wallets—
The end of the price of admission.

For them it's another day
Sweeping the galaxy free of dust
Bunnies—for that reason

The stone turns to a mirror
As it approaches and when it lands
No one can look away—
Ever—from one another's suffering—
Ever—you dig—
Again.

Poverty's Mansion

The count rides another
Horse to death then comes home
To his children asking if
They'd like to recite the lessons
Learned from beneath
The skirt of the current tutor.

I don't care if the skirt
Is calico or organdy but am aware
The dead horse was left
For servants to divide into
Equal portions for their families.

If I cry about anything
It comes from looking with two eyes
Open seeing only one thing—
The child on the banister
Losing balance as the parallax of joy
Becomes a head wound.

When we wake up in a painting
Of an empty stable where a bucket
Of rain reflects an eye not yet open
Let's surrender before it does.

Dynasty

I talk to the orchids on my kitchen
Counter most days—ask forgiveness of them—
Understand they are lost and far from home
And alone in alien soil with smells
Of meat in their stamens and dogs barking
And timers going off—I do my best
To make my world a jungle where they grow
Their pale flowers and die warm in the steam
Coming off kettles and dinner plates.

I can't look at anything anymore
Without seeing the bones under the skin—
The lips of the ventriloquist moving—

The hunger in everything wants out—
Held hostage to the coming bite—
I place the fallen brown petals in the unmarked
Grave of my poem where no one can disturb
The mad flowers of the exiled king.

Gratitude

This life—inside fur
Or shell—a pink nose
On a stem—under saddles or
Crossing bridges in hostile wind—blown
Apart—broken young—put
Together old—tender in places
Rubbed raw by touch—filled
With hope—a balloon lifting
In the night sky of the heart—
Wanting charity—generous with what remains
When charity is gone—ruled
Like drying paint by atmosphere—
Adrift—the sweet drip
Of love beneath a fatal marathon.

This life—its exact
Brevity—it's anticipatory
Romance with pain—its
Thorn in blue mornings
With rain on the point—

This life—private—shared—
Like sunset smeared on stones or
The acrylics of goodbye—

This life—ours—hurting—
Loving—shouting—sleeping—
Dreaming—pausing—permeable

To dark and light—transparent—
Blood beneath busy hands—pieces—
Waiting for the continuous application
Of attention that is a medicine
To make them whole—

This song—this minor
Key in the garden like spring
Flowers laughing under snow—
This song—

As long as it lasts—the sound
Of infinity humming in every mote
Of its trumpet—this us—these lyrics
Of touch and taste, the hemline
Of skirt—wet gloves by fire—

The cold lips with starlight
And chocolate—and tongue—
Words spoken—promises—
Kept and broken—the kiss
Of night and day the instant
They join turning gray—

Turning to twilight—or is
That morning light on the mountain
Beneath which an entire
Village of ghosts water
Their horses on human tears.

This life—this gift—this
Song—this moment—this us—
This never seen again *da kine*—

The tan lines where modesty
Builds a fence—the last breath
Of a child or sibling or lover—sound of leather
Soles slapping down corridors—
Drip of nectar in withered arms—

Or teakettles breaking
Wind—the second glimpse
Of gray in the mirror—the
Old inside the new—the crease
Where something was folded
In the night while sleeping—
The origami of the last smile
As it crinkles inside fire—

I look back and see it come—
I look ahead—see it come—
It's here—and so am I—
So are you—and the incidental
Darkness around this brightening
Gift of sight—this song—this
Bee in the closing petals
Of a rose—saying goodbye

To each season—to each redolent

Now where the beauty

Of the garden and the industry

Of the silent light come together in bone

Flowers to make the loud buzzing that

Awakening turns into honey.

Color of Gone

In the coda children go out in winter
To lie in the forest in solitary positions
Until they're covered by the insistent
Sweep of snow and falling leaves.

They hold very still as brittle-eyed
Wren flicker in the bare limbs like lewd
Inklings in the minds of nuns—fragments
Of winter sun on their throats—

Centuries later a child emerges
From a brush employed to paint a goddess
By dabbing various pots of cream—
She rules a self-actuated machine called
Memory from which the innocent are yanked
On to conveyors oiled by the pastels
Of diminishment—down to the engines
Fibrillating the blessed and the mild
Into believing unborn souls are
Shivering on the cold tiles of faith.

The prayers of summer trees are for the
Winter birds that, having eaten hawthorn
Berries—describe in songs explosions
Inside their chest where closed cylinders
Power blood up to the shotgun blast
At the tip of every moving brush painting
The inside of the body red in order to fuel

The limousine bearing the next sacrifice
Toward the altar underground.

Student Life

The power plant in the professor's
Beard supplies the energy to give
Seeming originality to his tired old saws
Concerning the death of republics
And the economies of love resulting
In aberrations such as romance novels
Or the neotenic appearance of diapers
In the wardrobes of old queens.

As his student I was enthralled
By the constellations of moisture coming out
With the adjective "lovely" used
To describe the gestures of Proust
Or the fiddle hand of Nero—
I learned early to sit far away
From bearded men of knowledge
When they spray.

One day a bird flew in through an open
Window and every student watched
Its frightened arabesques leave blood
Streaks and feathers at impact points with
The unpainted walls of the mind—

The professor—I kept my eyes
On him—arranged his hair exactly like the image
Of Kafka on the jacket of *Amerika*—

Then drizzled at length on the modern
Theory that Ahab used herbal creams
To stimulate the harpoon he flung at
The nearly extinct white whale.

Like the bird I left blood
On the walls trying to get out.

Song for Everyone

There are leafy plants
Around the edge of the swamp
Watching the pale white ghosts
Walk out of a snowstorm.

They appear to the plants
As smoke from the rinsed eye
Of a bittern weasels are interrogating
Before embalming its song in their song—
The personal way this looks to unshaven men
Under cardboard near a Sterno can.

The ghosts are lost. The plants
Have white flowers in early summer.
White as snow. White as ghosts.
White as the feathers on arrows
An earlier century aimed at us.

But this is now. Everyone has
Found their ghost. The quivers
Are empty. The arrows landed. Some of
Us are wounded. Some of us dead.
Everyone is shivering near a small flame.
This is the historical moment to take back
The country no one owns.

Old Clothes

The mountain is quiet.
Nothing steps forward to take
Credit for the rockslide
That begins when a tiny pebble
Moves by itself like a finger
On an amputated hand.

My husband is painting
The mountain when it falls down.
Honestly—he didn't
Quite capture the spectacular
Nature of anything other
Than the sunlight which
Shines these decades
Later on the canvas with the same
Luster as his eyes when the marriage
Ended with roses and fingers
Crossed inside a boxing glove.

It's enough to have strong feelings
For someone without allowing
Their tongue in your mouth.

I Dig Music

The end of the gardener's day
Is a song uttered in a devotional
Chant beneath a weary breath that if amplified
Sounds like a trowel entering dark earth
With a twist of the wrist—

It's the music of a courageous
Surrender—the sound of rain
Negotiating the bright color of something above
Ground in the dark with a root—

I'd not want any better
From the world or from death
Than to hear this song for even
One second after I'm gone.

Tacitus

Said to anyone who'd listen
That last time in the senate he noticed
The boils on the shoulder
Of all the pages were about to burst
Indicating war will break out where no one
But the locals expect it.

The signs in shop windows
Indicate a day is coming when merchandise
Including carminatives and feathers
From the one true stork will be given
Away—thrown in the streets for anyone
Without principles to admire.

Tacitus knew the end alive
In every thriving moment
Hides in history's kiss like a bite.

Didn't need the view from the balcony
To understand why wild birds
Don't land on emperors.

Shears

The lilies regret their roots
Keep them from escaping the scissors
In the pale fingers of botanists
Who indiscriminately murder
What they mean to preserve—

The pastor of the local church
Works part-time as an arborist—
Tells my father not to stake
The little tree—plant it deep—pack
It tight—let the wind teach it
How to stand upright—support
Kills self-reliance in the young.

Then my sister got polio
And the neighborhood helped
With the cost of stakes
For her legs—

She's fine now—she
Dodged the shears—
She dresses in steel-toed boots
When she dances just to
Show there's no limit
To how strong we are.

Drone

The veiled shape is a grandmother
To the young boys working beside
Her—packing stones from the field
On the journey toward subsistence.

Above them the Hindu Kush
Disappears behind storm clouds the color of
Milk in a metal pail.

The grandfather is grinding
Blades the way time sharpens
Distrust—the stones fall
From the mountains all winter—

Almost always at night—
The sound of them ganging up
On starlight leaves a musical note
Like jostled skewers.

There's nothing militant
Here unless the noise of a shovel
Is the voice of heresy—

The missile enters the poem
The way a horse defecates on an ant colony
Simply because everything is
Where it is when shit happens—

If I were writing this poem
I'd ignore the falcon hunting
What small life escapes the heat signature
Because it's pushed by million-year-
Old imperatives and unlike
Us it has no off switch.

This is where the poem
Fails—where all literature fails—
To thirst sufficiently to drink the last drip
From the cold faucet attached
To the executioner's heart.

The Apartment at the End
of Hope Is Vacant

My grandparents told so many
Stories about me—*before I was born*—that
The difficult birth was expected and when mother—
In bloody sheets—was driven away by coroners
The medics left red wheel tracks in the hall.

It's said grandfather put me in an
Orphanage before I was named.

He was a Mennonite bastard
Delivered in the hay with a dung fork
By parents who bent steel around
Wheels that would otherwise wear down—

They punished my mother for
The beauty of her blue eyes—any color
On the human form being vanity—an attempt
To dress up the perfectly restrained
Dirt with unexpected flowers that
Might bloom in the cheeks or call snakes
Out between the legs.

That's all yesterday's news.
Now I'm a grown-up child relieved
I don't need my fingers to count
The unexpected joys in a heart
Raised downstream from a stone wheel
That generates enough power from cold current
To make this light by which I'm seen.

The Ferry

On the shore there are cattle with egrets
On their backs popping ticks with the expression
Of tasters for an unpopular king.

Foghorns are calling on the river—
Beautiful and haunting—warning of deadly
Consequences from chance encounters—

A famous confederate general once said
War is a middling poor way to create new jobs—
I watch the ferry approach with the crew
Directing the boat toward shore in orange vests
Like marmalade spread on ghosts—
Think of years of unemployment—living in poverty—
A student of poetry—how the heart never
Recovers from the sound of a slamming door—

When the ferry arrives I find today
Is not the day to cross to the other side.

It's never too late to pick a hammer up
And swallow it—all the way down to the place
Where the nail waits to be driven into
The unfinished sculpture that once
Complete expels a tear.

Rhetoric's Bones

Out in the fields just
Before the moon breaks
Over the stony ground sending
Fractured white light
Into the eyes of horses drifting
Toward places where a
Rockslide tore down the fence—
A coyote howls a question—

The herd supplies the answer.
The rancher the solution.

And we who consume
Everything—not just the painting
But the frame—roll our heavy
Bodies down the mountain
To break apart another fence.

Scylla and Charybdis

Two sisters by a brook
Can't believe how golden the maple
Leaves are as the wind tears
Them from the slender—black
Limbs that—once naked—bristle
Like grandfather's beard.

Each one cups water
In both hands—looks at the reflections
Leaking through their fingers.

Our selves live in the brook—
Look up at the falling
Leaves—the golden sisters—at
The world where holy men
And women look back with birds
In their eyes and hair—we are
Alive in everything—like the child—
Its head in mother's lap—the waves on
Distant coasts erasing cities
While forgotten love songs land on

The white suet in the bird feeder—these
Dreams of nourishment—these teeth
Forming in a nursing mouth.

Shipwrecked in Denial

There's something about
A sickbed with a thin daughter
Roped with blue veins playing
With her fingers as if dealing
An invisible Tarot card—perhaps
The one not yet created
With red crows carrying linen
Rags above a battlefield—

There's a movement in every
Circle toward the perimeter—
Some call this gravity or calculate
The angle of spin to the outside
By the equations in a scream—

In the way an ear assigns
Historical importance to the cries
Of birds above a broken nest
The rancher in a pickup hits a pothole
And the jukebox loaded with cowboy
Songs falls out on the hard road.

Nothing changes—when the hired
Hands plug in the jukebox the bunkhouse
Fills with *The Song of Roland.*

Dominion of None

It's midnight and the cliffs
Above the small cabin beside
The silver river glow with the fanatic grin
Of a god obsessed with dentition—

The river lusts for rain—retreats
Just enough to strand a yellow leaf on
A gray boulder that is an altar
Where the moon is worshipped
For its feminine translations of the night.

Inside the cabin a cat is curled
On the beard of an old man
Asleep in woolies near the cold
Stove because the chainsaw broke
And at first the winter
Was warm enough to sleep rough.

If there is enough money to fix
The saw I'll feed the cat.

Gravity

The pain of never landing
Known to every exhausted bird
Comes finally to the stars.

The one in your hand—
The one in your life—the one
Breathing in your bed—

Is with you now—will always
Be with you—will shine—even when
No one's left to see.

Adieu

When the monkey fist
Atop his neck uncurls
It's as if forty years
Fall away and he smiles
At the nuclear launch
Of last hours closing on
His dissipated body—

When something is ladled
From one pot into another there's
Loss and gain yet there's
Also equilibrium in that
Wherever a thing goes it leaves
The weight of itself behind—
Nothing is unbalanced by
Departure or arrival.

She leans over him.
Kisses the familiar skin—
Breathes the unforgettable smell
Of the garden she loves—

The world spins around them—
There's no traction in the rearview

Mirror—the road behind
Is iced over and humped
With shapes of things once
More than only visible—

For his part he just stopped
In one place and began somewhere
Else—she didn't know that
Then—but she will.

Emperor of Oblivion

The bloodroot bleeds like a hand
Mistakenly chopped by miners digging in a carbon
Seam for diamonds—it bleeds
To remind us not to harden our
Hearts to importunities in the dark—

Reminds us the fox is in the bell tower
Because—exactly because—there
Are no trees left now that the soldiers
Have come and gone—so the hounds have
Chased it up the next highest place—

Which is to say there is a relative
No one has seen for generations rolling
Above us with her feet strapped to casters—

And I am aware we don't agree
About her gender—but I am telling you
I've seen her step through a wall with the fox
In her arms—whereas you only believe
Her parents had no daughter.

It's possible you also believe
The bell will never ring again but that's

A confession the interrogators
Extract from the missing clapper.

No one prefers the story leaking from
The rag used to bandage the terrible vacancy
At the end of the wrist—no one will
Forget the soldier with a litter of dead kittens
On his wound licking the broken pipes
Of the dry fountain—the soldier dreaming
Of citizens beneath the ground—the
Fox alert in tomorrow's high place—the rose
Waiting for the discharge from the portholes
Of a sinking man of war to mix with sunlight
To push out another fatal bloom.

War is what the garden grows
When left to the underground monks
In moleskin robes in wet tunnels
Who suck moonlight down the necks
Of winter grass to fertilize despair—

Fortunately rainclouds descend
From the broken promises of the dead
And fill the empty cups so the party
Dying of thirst is restored in time to
Celebrate what it means to love
One weapon more than another—or—
To really hide nothing from myself—what
It means to be unafraid of drowning
In the runoff from a secular pew.

Love lost its pince-nez
And crawls on its knees among
Night-blooming jasmine toward
The hedge where the bloodroot gashes
Itself to emend this story in red—

Love is nearsighted—can't distinguish
Her temple from the madhouse where
The lips of sedated generals command
Everyone to keep fighting—saying—never
Surrender—while smoking a doctor
Right down to the butt.

In a dark holler overgrown with hickory
A family of moonshiners watch the recipe
Passed down from generations drip from a cold copper
Tube to become more potent inside a thought—
How personal hallucination is invigorated
When prodded by the mind up short ladders—

The blue eye of the porcelain doll clicks
Open and in it we see the swirling cape

Of the ventriloquist attempting to make
An entire vineyard scream in purple.

What's forced out tells the fox it's safe
To leave the bell tower and go back

Underground where the orphans
Left in flag-wrapped bones light candles
In the eyes of all the forgotten creatures
On their journey into morning glories.

Self Employment

When the hermit found a glove
Wrapped around a magician's wand
He didn't expect the hand inside
To touch his face with affection—

The passing of the wand—like
The passing of a genetic quality—
Occurs when the only meaningful
Awakening comes after the stranger
Takes off her outer garments and leaves.

Now the hermit is prepared
To lead the revolution with his
Newfound stick—he walks
Directly up to a beehive
And gives it one good whack—

For his reward—the hermit
Lies down in a quiet place
And dreams angels fight with demons to
Lick the venom from his stings.

The Revolt of Everyone

Between her legs a laundry
Chute opens—dumping soiled
Linen by the bushel on the tops
Of her bare feet while someone
Applauds the restraint it
Takes her sisters not to scream.

This time the horror movie
Ends well with the crumbling
Old parts of the city restored
To partial glory by a giant lizard
With a degree in architecture.

But the laundry lies unfolded
All her days which befuddles
The padre who thinks
His only job is to keep girls
From wearing his robe.

I'm tempted to enter this poem
To correct the nomenclature but refrain
Just in time to allow it to say—
Behind the closed eye a ballroom fills
With men wearing pompadours
Greased back with muskrat oil
Practicing their curtsies for the
Morning they wake up in a dress.

It doesn't require a gun
Or a stone or burning streets
Or ethics piggybacked out
Of crowds of angry mourners—

Just one clear moment
Of involution—where the self
Turns back to its shadow
To admire the light momentarily
Obscured—where spectators push
Out their chests like hens
And leave behind eggs that once
Hatched become active participants
In the final struggle to come.

Maturity

All these little boys
In the neighborhood
Walking around in their mommy's
Clothes thinking how
Cool it is to be pretty
Without a single judgment
About gender rules—

Grown men cackle
Over fences—point at one
Or the other and say things
Like—there's a problem
In the making—

Headlines scream from stoops
About troops invading other cultures
To teach them what to wear—

Meanwhile some of us grow
Old and still enjoy our
Mother's point of view.

The Artifact of One Another

I walk around the easel
Like a top spins away from its still
Center—altering the clouds I
Painted using a yellow or white
Oil believing this is the color
Of clouds in this particular sky.

It's almost eggshell but more
Like milk but not—perhaps it's too
Much to expect to get it right—
Get anything right—with pigments
Made from residue of the dead—

Oh wait—a woman appears—
At first just a sketch of movement
Somehow feminine like the water—
Materializing in pink out of the blue
Like a sunset or perhaps a sunrise—
Settling on the waves—

In the drawn hand there's a shell—
It glows pink—well—more pearl—no—
Like the cloud it possesses its
Peculiar luminescence nothing
Like the color on my brush—
When all the old lost light
In the universe suddenly pours out
Of our painted world to comfort the lost

Child rolled by memory like chicken
Necks in flour—I close my eyes—
Feel that same unfinished woman
Coloring the man inside.

Trade Beads

The mummery of the many
Resulting in laws passed
To protect the ermine-lined
Purse or to research the brace
Under the chin that keeps the nose
Out of the blancmange just before
The annual summary is
Read out loud by long-distance
Robots to a room of men so old
They believe their penis is simply
A new unpleasantness for
Cosmetic surgeons to address—

These gatherings where native
People are not present—where
No pine forest drops needles
Or fills the air with scent
Of owls and rain—where babies
Are dividends countries willingly
Prematurely withdraw—

Across the planet rivers dry up
While the water cooler promises rain.

The Ogre

1

I wake in a field no one
Remembers once expelled yellow
Buttercups like the first
Flush in gangrenous wounds—

I don't mean to offend—it's
Just that stripped of context
All colors are beautiful.

There's a bumblebee made huge
By insecticides carrying a baby elephant
Back to the hive—the elephant
Lives inside a cloud of yellow pollen—
Trumpets warnings of extinction
As winter strips its hiding place—

I think of Proust drooling
A morning absinthe into a napkin
Held by plump nurses who hate
Him for such an extravagance of velvet.

Let's say the field is greener
Than it appears in this poem—
Decorous with the black uniforms
And beards of passing shadows—

The trunks of elephants waving
Above the grass like gray knouts
Or big bore rifles made of chalk.

Let's say awakening hurts—

Let's say the effort to turn
Away is equal to the effort
To keep looking—holding buttercups
Up to the stars like monks eating prayers
Escaped from stone tablets—

Let's say the ogre is anyone
Damaged by anyone enough
Times to be physical to flowers.

2

In the same field winter
Arrives banging snow against snow
Like pedants clicking tongues
At resourceful students—I'd
Like to say I respected my teachers
But like winter I came

Late and stayed too long
To leave a good impression.

The classroom of each
Season is where professors of darkness
Meet apprentice shadows
For the purpose of entangling
Their familiar opacities.

The baby elephant learns early
To escape the baroque nursery
Where the copulation of the sublime
And the ordinary leave behind a sunrise
That is a scented opus in death minor.

3

The wolves that are free—
The wolves that debone
The husbands of the thick women
Running pell-mell from Cossacks riding
Through the buttercups as they herd
Livestock into a killing knot—

The wolves so ephemeral their shadows
Erupt like bad breath from skeletons—

Chew on the ogre long enough
To awaken him to the danger represented
By pages turned by an incidental
Wind such as an author exhales—

Not even the woman with her dress
Over her head imagines that in the house
Where she was born a childless couple
Oppose the appetites of false prophets
By painting the nursery black.

The only candle providing
Enough light to read this poem
To a curious Rilke looking up from the dirt
With eyes like buttercups filled
With snow turns out to be a
Fallen firefly emitting stored
Daylight from its wounds—

4

In the field the ogre sits in zazen
Biting the heads off flowers
Then sucking the secrets of the earth
Up the stem into its mouth like a
Fruit tramp drinking from a hose.

This is who we are—
All we are—at every moment
Boarded by dead passengers
Who don't care where we're going
But only want to rest awhile near
A red fountain and taste the rain
In the goblet of our open mouths.

Visitor

Visitor—if you are tired
Of the dry and patchy
Green lawn seen through
The yellowed lace curtains
Of memory so clearly reminiscent
Of cats pulling blue ribbons
From a wound that you describe in somniloquies
While napping beside my body—
Perhaps it's time to awaken—

Or maybe we're both tired
Of the wind distilling dirges
From the sad owls that starve
On bare limbs to the sound
Of winter breaking branches—

The room is heavy with gas—
Like trench warfare reduced
To killing furniture or a salt lick
Drunk on residual slobber
Breathing oceans at the stars.

You sleep and mutter how once
In Heidelberg you were cut twice by the Schläger—
One cut near each temple—by the master
Of the blade who was so hungover from
An evening with academy touts
That—like a novice—he placed the scars

Too close to your ears—too far
From the eyes for manly beauty.

A world can hinge on the proper
Timing of an injury—the arranged
Marriage with a wealthy heiress to
Save your father the disgrace of bankruptcy
Ended by misplacement of a cut.

One day we will change places—
I will sleep in my bed and you will move
Around me—arranging red flowers—
Placing them soberly—careful not
To disturb this dream which as you know
Will be all that's left of us when
The gas leak is discovered.

Caste System

I'm grilling bush meat
Over an open fire made of animal
Stools mixed with river
Grass—it's perfectly hot
And illuminates a circle
Within which my family waits
For the meal to slide
Off the scavenged fence post
Impaling the monkey.

Kabir said the beloved is in
Everything and he knew this
Better than most having
Turned so many cheeks as a child
His brown face grew red
From hands that slapped
Him into poetry—

I tell my family—
The monkey is ready.

Texas Two-Step

I want to speak—but people
Are praying so loud to gods
That obviously don't listen
Or the people would be—well—more
Attractive—that I can't think of anything
To say—it's not like me to snip one flower
In the fragrant garden fertilized
By the decay of rotting thoughts—

These people pray with the gusto
Of someone passing a stone—

I silently float along through
My internal discord—beneath
The meditation on penance
Known to every rose growing
Its first successful thorn—

There's a creature at sunset mistaking
Last light for the end of time—subsequently
Making soup of their life in order
To drain the broth into a cry for help—

No. That's not quite true.
The urge to pray is more a painted mime
Saying nothing but conveying
Every suffering known
To the autumnal leaf—

The last person to leave the tent
Is the matronly sergeant at arms
Tasked with using her baton
On non-believers and barking
Dogs—whose yellow panties
Show above her uniform skirt
Like a smuggled daffodil—

Tonight it's all I can see—
The caution light in the fog—
This yellow flame in the soundless
Dark where old faiths deodorize
Their feet and gargle with mint before
Touching the wounded strangers.

Fox Hunt

I hate the little trousers
That buckle at the knee Pappa
Makes me wear atop the fractious
Pony—the chestnut mare—
I rode all through childhood between
The enameled holly trees whose red
Berries fell at certain times like
A clock dropping dead hours
On the ground that when mixed
With rain turn back into trees—

I'll not forget the last movement
Of the second hand before the alarm
Frightened the fox from its hole—

The big roan hunters snort blue
Steam in the cold air—the fox
Trembles in its lair—the golden
Color of Pappa's hair as it falls
On his shoulders which he brushes
Back with the barrel of his gun—

I'm the oldest son I say
To myself as the fox is torn to pieces
By the hounds and the men
Take the hedges with fiery eyes—
Boots flung sideways in the stirrups—

What anyone does next will cast
A spell on every day to come—
Will lift the dress of courtesans
On an ancient street so that children
Will begin to grow old—

I unbuckled my trousers
At the knee—no longer my father's
Child—lead the little pony back
To the stable and spend the years
Cleaning her stall—over and over—
In hope devotion to another
Will erase what I believe.

Landslide

Outside the window glass—
So old it bubbles with blower's
Breath—the view of an old uranium
Miner is partially obscured so we
Understand if not actually witness
Her opening both hands to set
A luminous woodpecker free—

Every clock in the house
Is rewound by the sun—even
So the woodpecker sits atop its nest
Timing the dead lice falling from its
Feathers like radioactive snow—

The miner lives in darkness
In tunnels she dozes through the earth
By changing expressions on her face in
The way smithies hammer red-hot
Tongs to pull ice from a bucket—

Speaking of ice—that's where
This poem lives—frozen in the highest
Remaining glacier—waiting for climate
Change to bring it down.

Rolling Stone

Snow covers the meadow
Which in moonlight looks
Like the pale bottom of a lost
Baboon caught in a fence or a frozen
Lake with swans stuck on it.

The dark trees holstered
In the drifts could at any
Moment fly away like sleeping grouse
Shot from hollow logs—

Not sure what to do next?
Then leave no tracks—violation
Of the sacred road is not requisite
For walking it.

When the door to the temple blows
Open notice the wind never stays
To worship anything—

Prefers its own company
To the momentary thrill of lifting
The skirts of lost angels.

The Bathysphere

For Incredulous the Third

The falcon returns to the wrist
Of the king with a duck wing beautifully
Plumed on one side and pink
With white bone on the other—

The duck survived and traveled
Years in the wilderness with one
Wing by excelling at alternatives—
Living on the ground—pestering
Mammals for handouts—picking lice
From their fur for food in the same
Way servants scrape grease
From a plate in the kitchen.

In this moment a stagehand
Moves the head of a stag to a wall
Where the lighting optimizes
Its indignant glare—the stagehand
Is named Matilda. She remembers
Her father bringing back meat
With horns for carving into buttons
Her mother stitched to a dress—

The meat never looked back
At her so she avoids the eye of the stag
When mounting it just right—

What isn't available because
It lives under her dress is the horse

80

Matilda rode to school with
Her little brother on the back
Farting with each step—crying
That he is shitting himself in
The saddle—on the way
To school the lessons begin.

Now the lighting is perfect—
The audience is waiting for the curtain
To open—and the empty seats
Applaud the loudest when it does.

The descent into normalcy begins
At the end of a tether outside a saloon
Where men in black suits and white
Shirts entertain penguins with stories
Of how to attract a mate—

When we sink into things—when
An arrow sinks into meat—when a fly
Sinks into amber—when fire sinks
In blue water—when tongues sink
Into mouths—when a calligrapher's
Brush sinks into an open wound
And renders a red owl carrying a blue
Vein through a moonlit forest—

When the last child
Sinks into the last embrace—

The empty page glares back at
Those who come to murder it
With words.

Leda

Every night since the dream
Began—since the door in the air
Tore open and glittering hooks
Pulled her from the icy sheets—
A lover comes in her sleep—

It starts with a slow, violet flicker
Between sensations of touch and taste
As if acid rain from a metal roof
Froze inside a purple drain—

Then pressure on the bed—a
Weight in the air above her body—
Wanting to land—shelter for
The tired wings—opening and closing—
Slowly—settling on her—heavy—
Like a cloud with an anvil inside—

It moves into her—not in one place—
In all places tired of resisting—
Until the weight of it belongs—until
She is one with it—large with it—

Until the sinking into her body
Is the flame of a candle guttering.
She bolts upright in bed—seeing
Daylight in an unfamiliar room—
She's caught in an understanding—

Intuitions migrate through blue veins
With luggage timed to explode—

Farmers on both sides of the fence
Gather around the swan believing
It's trapped in the barbwire—they set aside
Disagreements about pesticides—risk
The flailing wings—the yellow
Beak—to free something—to say—once—
They set something free.

When the swan flies away the world
Shrinks to the radius of child's moon-shaped
Face looking over a mountain under
A dress—the farmers take turns tearing
Down the goddamned fence.

Both Are Burning

It's not necessary
To speak crudely to convey
Worthy sentiments regarding
Disaffected anatomies and the
Knothole each gender
Uses to view the same game
On the other side of the fence—

Sure—you can tell they dodged
The price of admission by charcoal
Smudge around their eyes—

It's not about the way
Men and women size
One another up like tailors
With three-legged clients—or
Even the face of the moon
That no matter how brightly
It occupies the night keeps
Its dark side turned away—

It's the idea art can make
Anyone happy—this is—rather—the job
Of crafting useful things
Like silver peace signs or pastel
Swirls in frames or a cigarette burning
In a rented room where organic
Pillows are crushed by knees.

Art is not conversation piece
Or remedy for current or past failures
Of relationships that transplant the same heart
Back and forth between one body.

Art is just right now—like
The song in the guitar or the snow
On the roof—dripping one seasonal
Note while ravens circle overhead
Imitating people in love.

Black Rainbow

In a room heavy curtains
Cover all the windows—organ
Music drags a corpse into the ear
As if death is a song played
At half speed.

Even at noon this room is dark.
There's a stone pool in the middle
Reflecting candles in black water—

A single bubble comes to the top—
Bursts with the cry of winter birds.

Something loved is down there.
I reach deep into the pool
And pull its body up and spend
My life reviving her.

Only after she breathes do I
Understand she didn't want saving—

This is the hardest part—to let what
You love most go forever into the black
Night so they can live again.

Diffusion as an Engine of Chance

When in the course
Of life one is saturated
With headlines and grim
Repairs—when eviscerated by despair
Or drunk on accidental joy—
Go to the library and take down
Blake or Shakespeare and swab each
Wound with the author's gift—

Or go home to the record
Collection—take out Rachmaninoff's
Piano Concerto No.3 in D Minor—
Play it loud as you can bear—overwhelm
The room—the senses with sound—
Become the images of landscape
Hidden like pixels in a cathode scream—

Until the piano diffuses into horses
Running under crimson sky across
Barren desert from wolves—until
The volume of sound produces details
Of a trestle in the foreground—a trough
Filled with green water and a train
In the brown distance—its cowcatcher
Layered with bones and neckerchiefs.
There's a saloon door in every
Thing banging open and closed
In a dry wind—

Don't be afraid—it's okay to suggest
Fear is present since together we hung
It on a hook in a shared closet—

Go to the speaker—put your ear on it—
Turn the sound even louder—
Listen—this is the music Rachmaninoff
Heard—it's the raw edge of consciousness flickering
Between forms—it's bats at twilight
Pulling tendrils of black fur through purple air—
It's medics around a soldier under mortar fire
Clamping a vein—it's your first breath—
Long forgotten—that shot you from cradles
Like human cannonballs—

Is it safe to be so available
To one another's deepest sound—
Is it safe to descend without lifelines
To the bottom of the trench where
We begin—knowing the ascent will
Make us crazy with love for one another—

Is it beautiful here—or there—or
Anywhere—and if it is—can we stand it
Long enough to see it's a mirror
And not a lake where we drown—

Is it what the artist intended
Wrenching the bones out of his body—

Putting them back together
As a solid wall of permeable desire
Separating song from the creatures
Who shiver in caves and howl?

Is it what one hopes to receive
When folding a program beside perfumed strangers
As the crescendo begins—

Listen—crawl inside the sound—it
Is always true that we are inside
The best of one another—formless—
No bodies—just the art of creating
Bodies as they spin through dust—is
It still beautiful—does the pianissimo
Still run up the spine with the touch
Of wasps stinging a spider—

Or does it hurt—

Somewhere vague and awful inside
The bones—in the organs—in the temple
As it trembles before it falls—is it terrible—
All this amplified beauty—notice—the staircase
Upon which the sound climbs—the silence
Before each moment at the step—the silence
That is the skeleton dancing in the garden
Of pale blooms offering their last
Drop of blood to winter—to the ground—
To the next generation and the next—

The silence where everything sits
Like a stone on a steep cliff before
Ancient urges make the mountain
Shrug it off—and it falls like music on fire
Down slope—tinkling—echoing—hollering—
Smoking—burning—lighting up the night—
Producing every note it knows to describe
How against all odds we come to love one
Another in a nest of blue veins—

How to hold this precious world—this
One finger still—while the other hand
Pounds the keys—to love the bright
Magnitude illuminating the natal
Headlands of original fear—

There is an opening in everyone
Into the stars—a funnel where one falls
Into another—increasing speed
Until like the dislodged stone on the mountain
We land at the base of the sound
And rest in the same first chord—

The same silence—the same moment
Before the conductor brings down
The baton and the music—the heartbeat—
The powerful first movement—begins.

Treaty

Somewhere in Kierkegaard's
Vision of warmth there's a solitary heron
Flying above a saddled mare on her side giving
Birth to the sadness inherited by drinking
In the same river where ghosts wash
Away little remnants of the world still
Caught in their lustrous hair.

The point of this slow sifting of details
Is to question the reality we agree
Allows the insensitivity of failing
To provide the mare with straw—or—at
The very least—to take her saddle off.

In an impeccable movement the violin
Rises out of the cacophony of twigs drumming
A window in the wind to describe
Without words the sunlight on the face
Of the last caretaker holding a candle
Up to the sun—deciding if now is the time
To blow one of these lights out.

Lodger

There's a man eating from a tin
Plate sometime in the past or future
Around a campfire next to the opening
Of a shelter made from cedar
Poles peeled with a sharp rock and
Then covered by green boughs
To keep most of the rain out—

The man is dirty as a jester's
Sock and smoke from wet wood
Causes his eyes to brim with tears—
Unless he's crying because the meat
He eats was his only friend—

Someone's sons and daughters
Are looking down from trees
Where they feel safer than
On the ground—the man is using
A stick to pry loose a part
Of his memory still living
In the luggage of a villanelle—

Over and over again—the two
Refrains—like the crossed eyes

Of his wife—saying not what
They see but what they don't.

Eventually the trees
Are so filled with people
Afraid of the ground—scrambling
For the highest branch—the forests
Convulse and throw them off.

No one remembers what
The fortune tellers said comes next—

Except the dinosaurs.

Last Night with Krishnamurti

I waited for the room
To darken before spilling
Violet-scented water in a tub
For my swollen feet.

While soaking each toe
I pared the skins from eggplants
All purple and black into
The water where they turned
Light blue as a fascist eye—

If there's anything in the mail
Or on my stoop when I wake up
I'll leave by the back door
With my eyes closed—through
The yard where the rooster
Is afraid of the sun.

There are appointments.
This is an appointment.

If Anne Boleyn carries her head
In her hands while weeping
For a lost love that blew out the windows
Of her face like manikins escaping
The probe of the designer's hand—
May we then presume to exchange vows
With someone looking into our eyes
With the sincerity of a moonlit owl?

Speaking of birds—in a rain
Forest drying up from thermal
Pressure introduced by fire
Retardants and perspiration
Creams the last of an ancient
Species sits atop
Its nest on an egg cold as tile
On the floor of an igloo—

This is love—this is hope—
This is the cost of a vigilant heart.

Grand Paw

You hide in the bushes
All day until night comes
Then wallow in the shadows
Cast on the lawn by lilacs
As if the darkness in your blood
Found its birth place
Behind a picket fence.

This is the promise of night—
Obscurity—private indulgence—
Religious excitements—personal
Breakthroughs in oral hygiene—
The sacristy of a backyard
Filled with the holy light of stars
And the antics of a child
Giving way to morning when
The vessels are emptied
In a trough and moistened
By the expectorations of duty.

So it goes—each generation
Coming out only at night to hear
The messages wrung from the silence
Of the broken toys.

It

It cajoled and beckoned—
Prayed and cursed—it
Opted to say thanks and spat
On any gratitude—it sang
In every cell and was quiet
For a million years—it listened
To the rain and wallowed
In desert sand—

It did everything and nothing—
It lived in everyone until they died
Then lived in death until death
Died then put all the pieces
Back together and lived
And died and lived again—

It fingered its ear—it
Rubbed its chin—it held
Babies up to the moon—
It rode blue herons
Into the stars like light—
It rode light into darkness
And kept riding—

It grew awesome
And insignificant—
It paled when tired—
Radiated with vigor—

Still it was alone.

It curled under a stone
And waited for the planet
To grow a fiery tail—

It gave up on society—
It shook shook shook its booty—
It lost hope for friendship—
It whimpered like a saxophone
Played by the wind—it took
Notice of nothing but solitude
From which shadows
Formed on a trellis of bones—

It cross-dressed well
Enough to win beauty pageants
In five of the seven genders—

Still—it was alone.

There were other its
In other places also alone—
Its are always alone—

When they come together
We and you and them form—company
Happens—wars happen—terrible things

In the name of companionship—lovely
Things as well—all terrifying—all
Inevitable when it is not alone—

So it chose—
Chose to be a tent peg—
To hold fast in the hurricane—
Invisible with unseen but felt influence—
It is there—it is here—

It's in you and not—
Around you and not—
It's the first pulse
From the new heart—
It's the last pulse of the old—
It's forever inside forever—
It's the only right now—

And it is gone.

Atonement

Nothing is less worthy than
The hatchet-faced man momentarily
Drowning his naked daughter
In a muddy river while the choir
Dances in clogs atop a platform
Of green planks wired to straw.

The wooden shoes on the wooden
Boards could be coconuts falling on a beach
Crawling with marooned puppets.

One ecstatic trips on another
And falls on the bone erupting from
Page seven in the book of fallen leaves—
It may be actually read at some point
But for now the page is content
To impale anyone who believes in it.

The child is unsaved until it
Survives the ritual dousing. There
Are dead willows along the banks
Condemned to endlessly remember
Winter breaking all the windows
In the derelict temple where gloved hands
Play the frozen instruments.
The child flops out of the grip
Of the man with a face like an ingot
Of iron and swirls away downstream—

In another universe she surfaces
Beneath a glass ceiling and breaks
It with both fists so the just men on the other
Side have no choice but to allow her
Presence to erase them.

Winter

When the snow melts a small
Lake forms in which a hobo drowns
By rolling down its banks after
A spiritual flogging by thunderbirds—

We all opened our gates
And tried to revive him—
It was suspected he was someone's
Lost father hung inexpertly
On the scaffold of hard miles—

Either way no one spoke.
We watched all summer while
The body was reclaimed by thorns
And the verdigris of looking away—

We watched the sun roll over this
On its journey toward winter—

Which came just in time
To freeze the lake for as long as it takes
To drown the cries of meadowlarks
Trapped under the ice like an elevator of mutes
Between floors in a burning tower.

Framing the Question

Even after seventy
Years of actively disliking
Him she was never
Unkind to his dogs.

Alone on the stoop
With the bottle tree chiming
Prayers each time the wind blows,
She asks forgiveness
From herself and receives
It in time to understand
Loneliness is a blessing.

The restraint of one woman
Over the course of a life
Spent with the wrong man
Can be summarized
By extracting Atlantis
From her tears and rebuilding
It in a thimble of salt.

Games

In this war the innocent
Are in charge and so don't
Believe the bullets
And bombs are real but
Instead believe the dead walk
Away when the game
Is over—but in reality

Nothing moves or speaks
Once captured in a sad refrain—
Except the white flags scattered
Like broken promises by angry winds.

Courier's Lament

We're precious in our lavender
Cloak and waxed moustaches—
Just so—the reek of atomized
Laurel on the neckerchief—prelude
To holding the chair for the queen
Who enters the banquet like a nautch
Dancer in burlap—her pince-nez firmly
Affixed to bosom and nose.

I am the ideal of my times.
I hold the epee with the wrist
Anticipating in its limpness
The sudden thrust—or the brush
Held in a similar manner when
Rendering a bowl of purple plums
From a pot of tinted oil.

For reasons undisclosed
The summer palace is closed
This year. The servants
Sweep leaves and insects
Off the pavilion mats but no
Hands wrap a glass or pluck
An errant eyebrow hair.

We live alone all our days—
Like ghosts in boats bailing
Speechless incantations into

The ears of those deafened
By huge waves of presumption—

Offer our small flame to one
Another with the expectation
The end is merciful—perhaps
Meaningful—bells ring in the distance—
A nightingale floor creaks
With no one on it—only shadows—

Walking dark corridors
In atrocious garb reflecting
Back the decorative spirit of the times—

Like a mirror drug down
A cobbled lane in late winter
With a raven flying in it—
Fleeing acquisitive minds.

The Model

The revenue stamps issued by the lords
Of the city state of Hessen Cassel were embossed
With lions before the Prussian army
Tore down the castle and ate the cabbages
Staring at each other like drunken spectators
Who've forgotten their names.

When the Prussians annexed the rivers
And the stone waterwheels—the millers were forced to grind
The wheat into bread with the tips of bayonets
Pressed one centimeter into their ribs—children
Who witnessed this voluntarily gathered
Lilies to place under their pillows before
Dreaming of leather figments in the sky.

The new revenue stamps were embossed
With eagles by the conquerors in their steel
Helmets with spiked tops who played a game
Where they tossed their hats in the sky
So they'd fall point first on something.

In the salon the jewel in the eye
Of the mounted rhino watches the sheiks
On their golden yacht in a blue ocean
Say goodbye to their brides strapped
To anchors before pushing them into the sea
To insure there will always be oil . . .

Hold still says the artist to this poem—
Used as a model for a pastel statement
About growing old in the post–dark age room
Where the lights come on when we leave—

Hold still—or I'll get it all wrong.

Guidance

By leaving everything to chance
The shaman lost his job
And the tribe flourished
Under the leadership of a child
Who ignored the movement
Of stars and the pattern of blood
From a neck wound or the
Animal tracks on fresh graves—

And pointed south—said—
"There—it will be warmer."

Then the northern migration—
The circle of one people—came
Into contact with the southern
Lodges and the circles overlapped
And the children whispered
To one another in the dirt
While the elders endlessly
Brokered a lasting war—

Thousands of years passed
Before anyone thought to
Look in orphanages or nurseries
For the secret way out.

Ambulance

The thing on the stretcher
Carried by medics from the burning
Village is dreaming angels
Are lip-syncing hymns while
Lashed by an invisible scourge—

The actual angels attending
Dream the thing on the stretcher
Will die so they can stop coveting
The exquisite brevity of its pain—

None of this matters because
No one is really dreaming because
No one is actually asleep.

Dark Hunger

Universes eat fire—
Spit new stars from rejected
Matter that clots into planets,
Asteroids, lap dogs—and yes—
Pogo sticks and Vaseline.

A little boy in an alley curls
Around a scooter that has no
More useful parts to steal
And lies discarded among
Curb angels who gravitate to
The metal because it stays warm well
Into the cold night.

When the new day comes
The boy washes in puddles
Left from a brief shower then
Staggers out of the alley into
The promiscuous touch of daylight
That illuminates nothing except
The future trying on old wigs
In pawn shop mirrors.

On the lips of the mime
Describing this—sorrow hangs
Like thunderheads
Above a playground—while
In the garden of mercy
The long draught continues.

Virtually

On the way to the big city
There's a stand of alders
That seems to go on and on
Along a back road
Where fertilizer trucks
And combines move so slowly
There's no hope of passing
One because another will
Be right there in front of it—

So you open the windows
And smell the fields
And duck when the shadows
Of crop dusters come
Out of the sun like a divine wind
Over battleships—

But the reason I mention
The poplars before going astray
Is because once a woman
In white like a Gainsborough
Nude only with clothes on
Appeared at the edge of all
That green carrying a basket
Of apples and leading
A chestnut mare by a gossamer
Cord that was not quite halter
And not quite leash. Not quite
Umbilical—not quite visible—

By the time this registers
I'm hundreds of miles
Down the road in a cheap
Hotel with a broken neon sign
Buzzing like a traveling electric
Chair—infiltrating my room
Through the closed blinds
With an organ-colored piece
Of a forgotten view—

A creature appears in the rearview
Mirror—yoked to this perspective
By a strand of ancient light—

It's pushing a wheelbarrow
Down the empty highway behind me—
Gathering trash from ditches to decorate
The interior of the next revolution.

In the Jungle

Seemed uncivilized to the pastor—
Reading from the gospel according to
Translation—that orangutans stripping
Figs from low branches paid more attention
To her orations than the grizzled farmers
In bib overalls nodding in their pews.

Let them sleep for now—if god
Is anywhere she is also
In their dreams luring
Them closer to a waterhole—

For now the sermon is about
How to avoid getting struck by lightning
Or deafened by thunder when the storm
Targets the place you sit busy
Folding the pages of your life—chapter
And verse—into kites no one
Believes will fly—until they do.

The Weight of Light

The knight looks out his visor
From atop a Percheron
Warhorse trained to ride through
Ossuaries at night so it doesn't
Spook when trampling an enemy.

I walk down the alley dodging
Hands that reach from dumpsters
Until I find a reasonably dry
Spot beneath a crumbled lintel
And sleep in my clothes.

There's a breath somewhere
In the world waiting for anyone
To find it—there's a dream
In every shadow of sunlight
Breaking through the dark regret—

I awaken toward dawn
With a child no one wants
Asleep in my arms.

Live Fast Die Young
Leave a Poem Behind

The sādhu tempted death
By breathing underwater just
Long enough to dream of fish
Love and the impossible mammalian
Birth of whales coming
Out of pink unfolding tissue
Into suffocating waves—

What is up with that hollers
The yogi at the bent trees whose
Shadow is not enough to shelter
One ant overheated from dragging its
Genitalia toward the queen.

Why is it so hard to awaken
The newly dead when just a moment
Before they were alive—maybe
Even curious about the way
Sunlight excarnates Sufi dancers
In an endless angle of repose.

Because they are not listening—
Says the corpse to the doctor.
They don't need silly inquisitions

And bloody dawns and operatic
Proclamations of frivolous despair—

They are not listening
To you anymore—they are listening
To the absence of you—which

Is a song in the way rain
On a scarecrow is a baptism absolving
Crows of their trespass.

They don't need air raid sirens
To tell them roses aren't red
By choice or that bird songs
So admired by poets are actually
The shrill objections of orphans—

Who—no matter how loudly they shout—
Can't get it through the world's thick head
That beauty is often the sword point
Of someone's pain.

Birdbath of Saint Francis

1

So much is happening everywhere—
All at once—like the wolves on the edge
Of the village chasing a small boy
Right up to a church then entering
The child to partake of the host—

Of course the birdbath is filled
With blood—or in some cases
Dry as a cracker representing
A soul with only the remnant sky
Crusted at the edge of stone.

All hope is rewarded one day
In the past—so the dead claim
As they flutter in and out
Of a bucket filled with dread—

The sparrow pushes his chest out
Like a recalcitrant hobo moved
Along by nightsticks for not having
The correct change in his pocket—

All at once I say—all at once—
The world is filled with particles
Of things that, after entering the temple—
Spray ghosts on the walls.

2

There's a man in bib overalls
Poking a muskrat hole with a pistol
In his other hand hoping to bring
Dinner home to his family shivering
Around a campfire near a bend
In the river exactly where the current
Exposes the roots of willows.

How does anyone expect grace
With mouths wet with desire for flesh
As beautiful as their own.

A voice for the league
Of immaculate reflection whispers from
The rain left in a yeti track
Where fables come to drink and bathe—

It speaks on behalf of the river—
In summary of all the tears cried

Over generations of membranes
Scooped apart by spoons—it says—

The river will tolerate no more
Campfires on its bank or families
So dire and needy they mistake

The night as a vacation from light and
Step upon the hidden bones in it.

A raft filled with poets shoots
The waterfall above the campfire and strokes
Quickly past the bank where
The family is roasting something
With sticks through its ears—

The poets are quiet as the raft
Drifts downstream through greasy smoke
But later write crude sestinas about
An afterlife spent on bicycles delivering
Nightmares to the stoop of dreams.

3

I think that says it all.
There's really nothing more to say
Without sacrificing meaning
To the blonde bombshell of confusion—
It's fear of endings that drives
Clarity to estivate in the cool mausoleum of thought
While books burn in libraries—

Except perhaps it's okay
To say I'd love to be whole again. I'd love
To see whole people—a whole planet—
Be safe from undesired touch—

I'd be satisfied though with
A sunrise that lasts forever.

4

Much to my surprise the poem
Continues while I drag the raft ashore
To clean it out before settling for
An evening with Auden—

"They built by rivers and at night the water
Running past windows comforted their sorrow . . ."

I feel nothing at all rowing upriver
Toward the fire between the willow roots
Where the family sings along to the screams
Of a rodent whose tail twitches in ash.

The poem—like the river—
Never stops—even when everything
That drinks or bathes in it is gone.

The Wild Garden

The wind comes out of the north
Blowing before it the cold memory
Of a face so brave it never
Looked away from anything—

I see the chestnut trees sway
To the south as if migratory birds
Pull them along toward warm climates—

Today I climb the highest one—

I'm not a captain here—just
An ordinary sailor aboard a boat
I didn't build like all travelers on
Hard roads paved by innocence.

Today I stay in the tree
Until night comes and the moon
Touches my hands—it's autumn—
And like everything else
I hold my breath and let go.

Carnival

Like something with eyes pickled
In a jar behind a cowboy bar—
Or inside a circus tent in a meadow where
Dogs nip the ankles of peep
Show rubes—the saint
And the sinner share one heart
And two vistas—joined
Not by common destination but by
Language describing faith in existence
And non-existence as simply a prosaic river
With no visible banks flowing
From ignorance toward a reckoning.

The agreement with the opposite
Voice at any given moment of decision
Comes at the expense of an afterlife
Not outside but inside the body
Where the celestial experience is
As simple as a cool glass of clean water
Dipped from the smile of a child.

Please tell me who said that—
I forget.

Herb Garden

About the time the priest rubs his necklace
While punishing the congregation in Latin—his memory
Is upset like a cart filled with ziplocked goldfish
Taken to market in a desert town known
For its figs and oranges and nomadic
Children born with extra fingers on one
Hand in the same amount missing on the other.

The priest stops in mid-delivery and giggles
At the simplicity of things when viewed
Through a cellophane bag—even the palm trees
Take on the ephemeral nature of a playground
After the bullies relax their hands.

People are waiting for assurances—
Assurances that the demon everyone says
Is courteous and gentle when extracting the soul
With tweezers is no longer running for office.

No one has sufficient memory to count
The blessings stored in the unfinished
Tower of childhood where geneticists try
To grow new hands from a buried glove.

The glove shrieks when pricked
By needles and smeared with cellular
Jelly before dipped in promises—

From deep underground the sound
Of one hand clapping begins.

Leaning Tower

In every letter written
By someone missing someone
There's a small gray bird
Longing for a place to land.

We can leave this story behind
Now that we have the bird
To point the way home—I
Know because following it
I ended up in this shy
Memoir in which it's possible to
Confess my love to you who
Willingly untie the dark ribbons.

And if tomorrow finally comes let
It be with one useful idea to help
Save the little we left behind.

Missile Crisis

The brown man from Pinar del Rio
Licks a crumb of tobacco from the tip
Of his knife before cutting
The perfect fart—perfect because
It disperses the tourists while endearing him
To his wife and children helping steady
The donkey pulling the cart
Filled with green wrappers down
To the factory for rolling the cigars
The region is famous for.

Now the tourists are fanning themselves.
The brown man says in excellent English—
"Ah—smell that fine tobacco" which
Causes his oldest son to giggle.
The man startles the donkey by farting
Again—saying—"all aroma is particulate
In nature" which amuses him
Until the donkey responds.

No one is improved by visiting
Shrines or countries where the industry
Of locals is mistaken for entertainment.

Modern World

The ringworm on the neck
Of the revolutionary resisted
All treatments except the axe.

Modern world—if it seems
To you I am less respectful
Than a cigarette smoker to a lung—
Be aware—the snow falling
On your neighbor's eyes
Is helping his cataracts—which—until
Now—prevented him from seeing
How much cruelty there is
In the pocket of his favorite suit—

I am done with everything
That showers in the spittle of the sky—
Done with the wild men
Under your dress who only
Come out when rewards are offered
For the escaped convict
Who murdered something there—

Maybe the century—it's been so
Long since a wanted poster

Looked anything like the criminal
Now hiding near a panty line.

If anyone is sane—it's me—
Leaving this world for the next world
In a wagon filled with words
Someone will braid into a prayer
That asks for nothing and receives it.

Amen.

Nowhere to Hide

When the gods you don't believe
In drag you out of your comfortable
Life and kick your ass long enough
And hard enough to make you
Question your serene acceptance
Of emptiness as the obligatory tyrant
Whose lack of moral concern is
Responsible for your largess—

It's time to wake up—take off
The bedroom slippers—put on the
Mud boots and go clean the stall
So the horses' feet don't rot—

Ride away with a gentle agreement
On your tongue that if loosed would
Sound like an apology but stuck as it is
Between molars is more like a curse
Chomped by inaction into an antidote
For clarity—the steam of a promise swabbed
From the smithy of cold eyes.

Be kind—love what you see—or go
To sleep and stop dreaming you're one of us.

Misunderstood

I get up every day
Stepping one foot then
Another out of bed
As if walking into the cargo hold
Of a ship bound for exotic
Jungles on coasts where arrival
Makes the coconuts fall
With a sound like boxers
Working a heavy bag.

When daylight is too
Bright the curtain comes down
Automatically—wired to
A synapse in the brain
That feels safe in a darkened
Room with pillows and unconsidered
Possibilities outside the door like
Coal beside a railroad track—

What is so disturbing about
An invisible body singing
An audible song.

Biographical Note

Gary Lemons studied for two years with John Berry-
man, Donald Justice, Norman Dubie, and Marvin Bell
in the Undergraduate Poetry Workshop at Iowa City
from 1971–1973. He has published five books of poetry,
including *Bristol Bay, Día de los Muertos, Fresh Horses,
Snake,* and *Snake: Second Wind* (the last two of which
comprise the first two books of the Snake Quartet).
For decades he fished Alaska, built grain elevators,
worked high steel and re-forested the clear cuts of the
Pacifc Northwest. Currently he and his wife, the artist
Nöle Giulini, teach yoga from their studio, TenderPaws
in Port Townsend, WA.

CPSIA information can be obtained
at www.ICGtesting.com
Printed in the USA
FFOW05n1826140317